TRUE CRIME

SERIAL KILLERS

T. R. Thomas

SADDLEBACK
EDUCATIONAL PUBLISHING

TRUE CRIME

SADDLEBACK
EDUCATIONAL PUBLISHING

www.sdlback.com

ISBN-13: 978-1-59905-436-0
ISBN-10: 1-59905-436-1
eBook: 978-1-60291-762-0

15 14 13 12 11   3 4 5 6 7 8

Photos:
Ted Bundy, Betmann/Corbis
Jeffrey Dahmer, Reuters/Corbis
Aileen Wuornos, Getty Images

CONTENTS

INTRODUCTION

There have always been serial killers. Vampire and werewolf myths may actually have been based on serial killers.

Today the number of serial killers seems to be rising. There could be as many as 350 in the United States alone.

A serial killer is someone who has killed at least three people. The killings take place over more than 30 days. There is a cooling-off period between murders.

Serial killers usually kill only one person at a time. But they keep killing. Often they have an urge to kill. That urge gets stronger until they kill again. They can't seem to control it.

There is usually a pattern to the killings. Some killer's victims are all boys or young men. That was the case with Jeffrey Dahmer. Dr. Harold Shipman killed mostly elderly women. They were his patients. Ted Bundy preferred young women.

Aileen Wuornos was a female serial killer. She was a prostitute who killed her male clients. The Green River Killer murdered prostitutes and runaways.

Serial killers murder for different reasons. For many killing provides a sexual thrill. Others kill for money or revenge. Some think God or a demon made them do it. Whatever their reasons, serial killers cause terrible damage to society.

DATAFILE

T I M E L I N E

Summer of 1978

Steven Hicks, 19, becomes Dahmer's first victim.

February 1992

The court sentences Dahmer to 957 years in prison.

November 28, 1994

Another prisoner kills Jeffrey Dahmer.

Where is Milwaukee, Wisconsin?

KEY TERMS

fantasize—to imagine something happening

homophobic—fearful of, or hateful to, gay people

indecent exposure—the crime of showing private parts to someone in public

infamous—having a very bad reputation

inmate—a prisoner in a jail or prison

DID YOU KNOW?

Dahmer murdered most of his victims at the Oxford Apartments in Milwaukee. Afterward the apartments were torn down. The site is now an empty lot.

JEFFREY DAHMER

It was May 30, 1991, in Milwaukee, Wisconsin. A 14-year-old boy wandered the street. He was naked and bleeding. He had been drugged and seemed out of it. Two young women saw him and called 911.

Jeffrey Dahmer, age 31, ran down the street after him. He tried to take the boy away. But the women stopped him. Soon the police arrived. Dahmer told them the boy was 19. He said he was his boyfriend. The police laughed.

Serial killer Jeffrey Dahmer makes his first court
appearance in Milwaukee County Circuit Court.

"We reunited the lovers," they joked. They made other *homophobic* comments. They thought it was just a lovers' fight. So they let Jeffrey Dahmer take the drugged boy away.

Soon the boy was dead. He was Dahmer's 13th victim. Dahmer kept the boy's skull.

Later police remembered a strange smell in Dahmer's apartment. But they didn't do anything about it. The smell was from the rotting body of Anthony Hughes. His corpse was in the bedroom. But the police didn't go in there. They didn't check Dahmer's record, either. They would have found out he had a criminal record.

A Normal Beginning

Jeffrey Dahmer was born in 1960. He was a happy toddler. His parents loved him a lot. The bubbly blond boy was curious and smart.

One day his father cleaned under the house. He found some animal bones. He dropped them into a bucket. *Clink, clink.* Four-year-old Jeffrey liked the sound. He dropped some bones in, too. *Clink, clink, clink.*

The family moved to Ohio when Jeffrey was eight. He became shy and kept to himself.

Jeff started to collect roadkill. He rode his bike around and picked up dead animals. He cut the animals open. He wanted to see what they looked like on the inside. Dead things fascinated him.

Once he found a dead dog. He cut off its head and put it on a stake.

A Twisted Teenager

Jeffrey got stranger as he got older. He started to *fantasize*. He imagined knocking a man out. Then he'd lie down next to him.

One day he hid and waited for a jogger to run by. He gripped a baseball bat. His plan was to knock the jogger out. But the jogger didn't go by that day. So Dahmer forgot about it.

His parents began having problems. Their arguing became yelling matches. They split up when Jeff was 17.

Fellow students said he was the class clown. He was always doing goofy things. But Jeff had a terrible secret. His urge to kill was getting stronger. He couldn't talk to anybody about it. So he drowned his feelings with liquor. He was an alcoholic by the time he graduated.

Dahmer's First Murder

It was the summer of 1978. Jeffrey was 18. He lived with his father.

One day he picked up a hitchhiker. Steven Hicks was 19. Jeff hit him with a heavy weight. Hicks died. Dahmer buried him in the backyard. He didn't tell anybody. It would be nine years before he killed again.

Jeffrey started college at Ohio State in the fall. But he stayed drunk all the time. He skipped most of his classes. He flunked out after one quarter.

"Join the army," his father said. Jeff did. At first he seemed to do okay. But army kicked him out after two years. They said he drank too much.

In 1982 Dahmer moved in with his grandmother. She lived in West Allis, Wisconsin.

Jeffrey stayed there for six years. His grandma had a hard time putting up with him. One day she found a gun under his bed. Police arrested him twice for *indecent exposure*. He stayed out late almost every night. There were awful smells coming from the basement. Finally she kicked him out. It was 1988.

The Oxford Apartments

After that Dahmer rented an apartment in Milwaukee. Later that apartment building became *infamous.* People knew Dahmer had done most of his killings there. So it was torn down.

Dahmer started killing more once he had his own place. By the summer of 1991 he was averaging a murder a week. He had become addicted to killing.

Dahmer found most of his victims at bars. He would take young men home with him. Then he'd kill them. Most were Asian or African American.

Often he did strange things to them. Sometimes he drilled holes in his victims' heads and injected acid into their brains. He thought that would turn them into "zombies." He wanted to keep his victims alive but unable to move. He also ate parts of their bodies. He wanted complete control over his victims.

Dahmer's Arrest

Police finally caught Jeffrey Dahmer. One of his would-be victims, Tracy Edwards, got away. Dahmer had threatened him with a butcher knife. Edwards punched and kicked Dahmer. Then he ran out the door.

Edwards flagged down a police car. The officers came to the apartment. Edwards showed them the knife Dahmer had tried to use on him. They found a human head in the refrigerator. They also found several acid-filled vats. There were human body parts inside the vats. There were also three more human heads and seven skulls. There was a human heart in the freezer.

Police arrested Dahmer and took him away. The date was July 22, 1991.

Trial, Imprisonment, and Death

Police charged Jeffrey Dahmer with 17 murders. Later they changed it to 15.

His trial began on January 30, 1992. The story was all over the news. People from all over followed it on TV. Dahmer wore an orange prison suit.

Jeffrey Dahmer claimed he was not guilty by reason of insanity. He argued that it was not his fault because he was crazy. The jury found him guilty. The court sentenced Dahmer to 15 life sentences. That was one for each murder. It added up to 957 years in prison. Jeffrey Dahmer said he was sorry for the killings.

Dahmer was sent to the Columbia Correctional Institution in Portage, Wisconsin. Another *inmate* attacked him on November 28, 1994. The prisoner, Christopher Scarver, hit him over the head with a heavy weight.

Jeffrey Dahmer died on the way to the hospital. He was 34 years old.

DATAFILE

T I M E L I N E

October 1, 1977

Hyde, England, welcomes a new doctor.

June 24, 1998

Dr. Shipman kills his last victim, Kathleen Grundy.

January 31, 2000

The court finds Dr. Shipman guilty and sends him to prison.

Where is Hyde, England?

KEY TERMS

cremation—reducing a dead body to ashes by burning

diamorphine—a legal type of heroin

exhume—to dig up a buried body in order to examine it

forgery—a fake document or signature

probate—laws having to do with the wills of people who have died

DID YOU KNOW?

Another British doctor was also a suspected serial killer. Dr. John Bodkin Adams was accused of murdering at least 160 patients. Like Dr. Shipman, he injected them with heroin. The court found him not guilty in 1957.

DR. HAROLD SHIPMAN

Hyde is a charming town of about 30,000 in Cheshire, England. Dr. Harold Frederick "Fred" Shipman started practicing medicine there in October 1977. He was a hard worker. He made house calls. Many other doctors didn't. His patients loved him.

He fooled everybody, though. Dr. Shipman seemed to be kind and friendly. But this was just an act. Police arrested Dr. Shipman in 1998. By then he had murdered at least 218 patients. The actual number may have been closer to 400.

Hyde is in Cheshire County near Manchester, England.

Many of his patients were elderly. About 80 percent were women. Usually they were found dead in their armchairs, fully dressed. Sometimes they were on a sofa or bed. They appeared to have died peacefully in their sleep.

The death certificate often listed the cause of death as a heart attack. Sometimes it was pneumonia or stroke. But what really killed them was *diamorphine*, or heroin. Dr. Shipman had injected it.

Things Didn't Add Up

Cab driver John Shaw had lots of regulars in Hyde. Many of them were older women. He got to know them well. Over the years he noticed a disturbing pattern. Many of his passengers were dying. Dr. Shipman was always involved. Shaw started keeping a list.

One day he dropped off a seemingly healthy lady at Dr. Shipman's office. She died right after that. Shaw was shocked. He showed his list to the police. By that time it contained more than 20 names.

Other people were becoming suspicious. too. Funeral director Alan Massey noticed that many people were dying unexpectedly. Many died in their armchairs. He knew that heart attack and stroke victims are usually found on the floor. Often they are trying to get to a phone when they die. Massey expressed his concerns to Dr. Shipman. But the doctor showed him the medical records. Everything looked fine.

Massey decided nothing was wrong. But his partner, Debbie, was not con-vinced. She spoke to Dr. Linda Reynolds. She pointed out all the *cremation* requests. Dr. Reynolds looked into the matter.

She was shocked at the high number of deaths. Dr. Reynolds contacted coroner John Pollard. The coroner asked the police to investigate.

Unfortunately the police said there wasn't enough evidence. They dropped the investigation.

A Forged Will

Angela Woodruff is a lawyer in England. She and the other lawyers in her firm specialize in *probate*. They decide whether or not wills are valid. Probate lawyers help carry out the dead person's wishes. They decide who gets their money and other belongings.

Angela's mother died suddenly on June 24, 1998. Kathleen Grundy was 81. Dr. Shipman filled out the death certificate. He listed "old age" as the cause of death.

Mrs. Grundy was a lively woman. She had worked for many charities. She had been the mayor of Hyde a few years earlier. The sudden death of this active senior came as a surprise.

A New Will

Angela had always handled her mother's legal business. That included her will. Mrs. Grundy had filed her will a few years earlier. In it she had left her money to family members.

Angela was shocked to learn there was a new will. It had been filed shortly before Mrs. Grundy died. Her estate was worth about 386,000 British pounds. That is more than half a million dollars. The new will gave all of her property to Dr. Shipman.

Angela could see right away that the will was a crude *forgery*. Someone had typed it carelessly. It contained many mistakes. Angela knew her mother had not typed this will. She had always been very careful. So Angela went to the police.

Police Arrest Dr. Shipman

This time the police had something to go on. The forged will provided a motive. Dr. Shipman had killed Kathleen Grundy for her money.

The police issued a search warrant. They were looking for the typewriter used to make the forged will. They found it. Dr. Shipman tried to cover his tracks. He said Mrs. Grundy had borrowed the typewriter. But the police found only his fingerprints on it. Mrs. Grundy's fingerprints weren't on the new will, either.

The police *exhumed* Mrs. Grundy's body. They found heroin in it. Dr. Shipman again tried to cover his tracks. He said she was a drug addict. Her medical records proved it. But he failed to realize something. His computer showed the dates he had made changes to the records. It showed he had gone in *after* her death and changed the file. He had faked the records of other patients as well.

Police quickly arrested Dr. Shipman for murder.

His trial ended on January 31, 2000. The court found Dr. Shipman guilty and sentenced him to life in prison. He hanged himself in his cell on January 13, 2004. It was the day before his 58th birthday.

DATAFILE

T I M E L I N E

November 24, 1946

Theodore Cowell is born in Vermont at a home for unwed mothers.

December 31, 1977

Ted Bundy escapes from prison in Colorado.

January 24, 1989

Bundy is executed by electric chair.

Where is Glenwood Springs, Colorado?

K E Y   T E R M S

decompose—to rot and fall apart

devastated—stunned, destroyed, overwhelmed

execute—to lawfully put someone to death for his or her crimes

extradite—to take a person to another state to be tried for a crime committed there

illegitimate—born to parents who are not married

DID YOU KNOW?

Ted Bundy told his mother all along that he was innocent. She believed him. One night he finally confessed to her that he was a murderer. It was the night before he was executed.

TED BUNDY

Stephanie Brooks is not her real name. But we will call her that. Stephanie was tall and thin with long dark hair. She parted it in the middle. Stephanie was a student at UW, the University of Washington, in Seattle. She was smart. She had big plans for her life.

The year was 1967. Stephanie started dating a fellow UW student, Ted Bundy. He was handsome and charming. They seemed like a happy couple. In 1968 Stephanie graduated. She moved to California. She

Ted Bundy leans on the Leon County jail wall as an indictment charging him with murder is read.

broke up with Ted. She thought he needed to grow up.

Ted was *devastated*. He couldn't believe it. Stephanie had been the light of his life. She was beautiful and classy. She made him feel complete. He couldn't stand losing her.

A Trip Back East

Ted dropped out of college after the breakup. He decided to take a trip. He had always thought there was something odd about his family. He wanted to find out what it was. He had lived in Philadelphia until he was four. But his birth certificate said Vermont. He went to Vermont to find out why.

The family secret was that Ted was *illegitimate*. His sister, Louise Cowell, was actually his mother. She gave birth in 1946 at a home for unwed mothers in Vermont.

Afterward she took baby Ted back home to Philadelphia. At that time people thought it shameful for an unmarried woman to have a baby. Her parents pretended the child was their son. They told everybody that Louise was his older sister.

Louise's father Samuel was a mean, violent man. Once he pushed Louise down some stairs. He also hated people of different races and religions. He kept a collection of violent pictures. Some people think Samuel may have raped Louise. They think he could have been Ted's real father.

Louise's younger sister Julia had a horrible memory about Ted. Once she woke up from a nap. Three-year-old Ted had taken all the knives from the kitchen. He had arranged them in a circle around her. They were all pointing toward her.

He was standing there smiling when she woke up.

Louise moved with Ted to Tacoma, Washington. Ted was four years old. She wanted to get far away from her violent father. She married John Bundy a year or so later. He adopted Ted and gave him his last name. But Ted and John were never close. John and Louise had four more kids. Ted often babysat.

Killing Spree Begins

Ted felt betrayed when he learned the truth about his birth. He began to hate women. He felt his mother had lied to him. He hated Stephanie for dumping him. He wanted to get even.

He went back to Seattle after his trip. He made himself very charming and smooth. He returned to college and did well. He even got into politics. In 1973 he saw Stephanie again. She was impressed. It seemed like he had really changed. He asked her to marry him. She said yes. As soon as she did, he dumped her. All he had wanted was to get even.

Young women started to disappear around that time. Many of them had long, dark hair parted in the middle. They looked like Stephanie.

A Sick Killer

Authorities believe that Ted Bundy killed at least 36 young women between 1972 and 1978. "Add one digit to that, and you'll have it," Bundy later told police. That means he could have killed at least 100. No one knows for sure. Even Bundy himself probably didn't know the exact number. He was addicted to killing.

Many of his victims were college students. Sometimes he attacked them as they slept. Other times he pretended to be hurt. He wore a fake cast. He asked young women to help him put something in his car. Then he hit them on the head with a crowbar. Once they were unconscious, he took them into the woods. He raped and strangled them if they weren't already dead. He kept the dead bodies hidden in the woods. He'd go back again and again to look at them. Sometimes he put makeup on their faces. Once they were too *decomposed*, he cut them up.

The End of the Road

Bundy tried to kidnap a young woman in Utah in late 1974. She got away and told police. But Ted Bundy was not caught until August 1975. Police pulled him over for driving strangely. The officer found his murder kit in the car. It included a ski mask, crowbar, handcuffs, trash bags, an ice pick, and other items. The police thought these were burglary tools. But Utah detective Jerry Thompson connected him to the kidnapping. The girl picked him out of a lineup.

The court sentenced Bundy to 15 years in Utah State Prison. But he was wanted for murder in Colorado. So he was *extradited.* They moved him to jail there. One day they let him visit the courthouse law library in Aspen, Colorado. He jumped out a second-story window and escaped. After six days police caught him. This time he went to jail in Glenwood Springs, Colorado. It was supposed to be more secure. He escaped again on December 31, 1977. This time he crawled out through an air duct in the ceiling.

Bundy went to Florida. He started killing again. He killed several women in

Florida. His last victim was a 12-year-old girl.

Bundy was tried for the Florida murders in June 1979. The court convicted Bundy. They sentenced him to death. Ted Bundy was executed on January 24, 1989. He died in the electric chair. He was 42 years old.

DATAFILE

T I M E L I N E

February 29, 1956

Aileen Pittman is born in Rochester, Michigan.

November 30, 1989

Aileen kills Richard Mallory, a 51-year-old businessman.

October 9, 2002

Aileen Wuornos is executed by lethal injection.

Where is Daytona Beach, Florida?

K E Y   T E R M S

appeal—a request for a new hearing

capital crime—a crime that can result in the death penalty

death warrant—a paper that orders that an execution be carried out

lethal injection—a method of carrying out the death penalty with shots of poisonous drugs

prosecutorial immunity—freedom from punishment, given in exchange for helping police prove a crime partner's guilt

DID YOU KNOW?

In the past, crimes such as rape or kidnapping could be *capital crimes*. In the 1800s a person could even be executed for helping a runaway slave. Today almost all capital crimes are murders. "Capital" comes from Latin. It refers to the head. In ancient times criminals had their heads cut off.

AILEEN WUORNOS

Most serial killers are men. About 15 percent are women. Usually female serial killers poison their victims. Many times they do it for money. Their victims are usually people they know. Often the killings take place in the female killer's home or workplace. Women don't usually get a sexual thrill from killing. Many male serial killers do.

Aileen Wuornos was a different kind of murderer. She was known as the I-95 Man Killer. Her killings were partly for money.

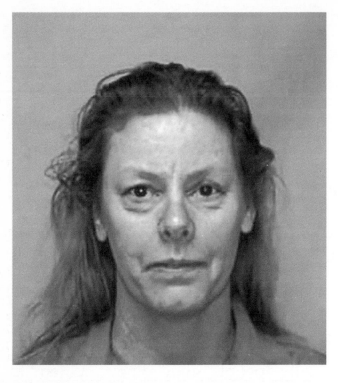

Aileen Wuornos is shown in this undated photo from the Florida Department of Corrections.

They were also partly out of anger. She used a gun. The men she killed were strangers.

In one year, Aileen killed seven men. She shot them along Florida highways. She picked them up for sex. She killed them instead. All the murders took place between November 1989 and November 1990.

A Rough Start in Life

Aileen Carol Pittman was born in Rochester, Michigan, on February 29, 1956. She had an older brother named Keith. Their mother, Diane, was only 14 when she married Leo Pittman. Diane divorced him before Aileen was born. Leo was in prison by then. He had raped and tried to kill a seven-year-old girl. In 1969 he hanged himself in his cell. Aileen never knew him.

In 1960 Aileen's mother abandoned her. She left Aileen and Keith with her parents. Lauri and Britta Wuornos adopted the children. Diane's father, Lauri, was a violent alcoholic. He brutally beat the kids. He molested Aileen.

Aileen didn't have many friends in school. Kids were afraid of her. She often had fits of rage.

Aileen got pregnant when she was 13. Her grandparents sent her to an unwed mothers' home. She had a baby boy. She gave him up for adoption. Her grandmother died shortly after Aileen came home. Then her grandfather kicked her out.

Life on the Road

Aileen was homeless. She survived by working as a prostitute. It was a hard, violent life.

Later Aileen hitchhiked to Florida. Eventually she met Tyria Moore. Tyria was the love of her life. By then people called Aileen "Lee." Tyria and Lee met at a Daytona gay bar. They were together for several years. Their relationship was stormy at times. Lee really wanted to keep Tyria in her life. But sometimes Tyria threatened to leave.

The Killing Begins

Aileen's yearlong killing spree began in 1989. Richard Mallory was her first victim. She picked up the 51-year-old businessman along the highway. She later told police he beat her and tried to rape her. Richard Mallory was a convicted rapist. But his record had been clean for a long time. She said he tied her to the steering wheel. He sprayed rubbing alcohol into her nose. He tried to rape and strangle her. But she got loose and shot him.

After Mallory she killed at least six other middle-aged men. She robbed them and then shot them many times. Some she shot in the back as they ran away. She stole their cars and dumped the bodies. Afterward she showed Tyria the money. She told her she was going to take care of her. She said they were going to have fun.

Lee and Tyria were moving from motel to motel. One day they were in a car accident. The car they were driving had belonged to one of the victims. Police found Aileen's palm print in the car. Witnesses described the two women to police. Police posted their pictures everywhere.

Caught at Last

Police arrested Aileen at a bar on January 9, 1991. Tyria had run away to her home in Pennsylvania. The police offered Tyria *prosecutorial immunity.* This meant she would be off the hook if she could get Aileen to confess. She called Lee. The police were listening. Aileen confessed so Tyria wouldn't get in trouble. She told the police Tyria was not involved.

Aileen Wuornos spent 12 years on death row. Her lawyers kept turning in *appeals.* They asked the judge for new hearings. Finally Aileen had had enough. She fired her lawyers. She told the judges she wanted to go ahead with her execution.

Florida Governor Jeb Bush signed Aileen's *death warrant.* He is the brother of former president George W. Bush. Only two women have been executed in Florida since 1848. Aileen was the second. She was executed by *lethal injection* on October 9, 2002. She was 46.

CHAPTER 5

THE GREEN RIVER KILLER

DATAFILE

T I M E L I N E

July 8, 1982

Wendy Lee Coffield, 16, disappears.

November 5, 2003

Gary Ridgway pleads guilty to murdering 48 young women.

December 18, 2003

The court sentences Ridgway to life in prison.

Where is SeaTac, Washington?

KEY TERMS

DNA—deoxyribonucleic acid, the building blocks of life

domineering—bossy and mean

meticulous—precise, fussy, thorough

plea bargain—an agreement where the accused pleads guilty to a lesser charge to avoid going to trial for a more serious charge

suburban—located in the towns outside a big city

DID YOU KNOW?

Dave Reichert led the Green River Task Force. In 2004, he ran for Congress and won. Reichert also published a book about Gary Ridgway. It's called *Chasing the Devil: My Twenty-Year Quest to Capture the Green River Killer.*

THE GREEN RIVER KILLER

Gary Ridgway seemed like an average guy. He drove a pickup truck. He lived in a suburban ranch house. Ridgway worked at the Kenworth truck plant in Renton, Washington. He had worked there for 32 years. His job was painting designs on trucks. He was very meticulous about his work. Coworkers thought he was friendly. They also thought he was kind of odd.

Some of the women at Kenworth thought Gary was creepy. They said he whispered nasty things to them. Then he turned red and walked away.

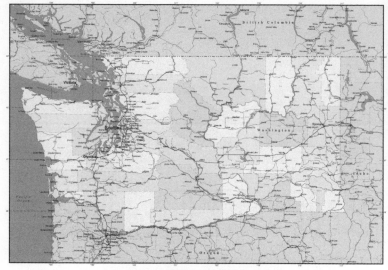

The Green River is in King County, near Seattle, Washington.

Ridgway's coworkers knew the police searched his locker in 1984. There was a huge hunt under way at the time for a serial killer. The police were leaving no stone unturned. They had 15,000 possible suspects on their list. Gary was one of them. But they decided he was not the Green River Killer.

His coworkers loved to kid him about it. They called him Green River Gary, or just GR. They had no idea he really *was* the Green River Killer.

Trouble with Women

Gary Leon Ridgway was born February 18, 1949, in Salt Lake City, Utah. He had two brothers. The family moved to SeaTac, Washington when Gary was young. Gary's mother was violent and *domineering*. She often yelled at the boys and their father. Gary wet the bed until he was 14.

Ridgway's IQ was tested at 82. This is less than average. He had to repeat a grade twice. He graduated from high school at the age of 20.

His murderous ways started early. At 16, he took a six-year-old boy into the woods. He stabbed the little boy with a pocketknife. The boy survived. He remembered Ridgway laughing. Ridgway said, "I always wondered what it would be like to kill someone."

Duty Calls

Ridgway got married right after high school. Then he went into the navy. He did a tour of duty in the Pacific. Often his ship would stop in the Philippines. Ridgway liked to visit prostitutes there. Once he got a disease called gonorrhea. He was angry with the prostitutes for giving it to him.

He went back to his wife after he got out of the navy. He learned she had cheated on him while he was gone. He divorced her.

In December 1973 Gary married again. His second wife was named Marcia. They had a good relationship in the beginning. Gary and Marcia often camped along the Green River. She knew all of his favorite places. Later she showed them to the police. Police found some of his victims in these same areas. Marcia said Gary liked to pretend to choke her. It got him excited.

Marcia gave birth to a son, Matthew, in 1975. After that the marriage went downhill. Gary didn't like sharing his wife's attention. Marcia left him in 1981. She was afraid of his temper.

A 20-Year Killing Spree

Two teenage boys spotted a body in the Green River in July 1982. It was a young girl. Her name was Wendy Lee Coffield. She was a 16-year-old runaway. She had been strangled with her own clothing. She was Ridgway's first victim.

Ridgway couldn't stop killing. He prowled the Strip. He was looking for prostitutes to pick up. Usually he took the young women to his house.

Gary had his son, Matthew, with him on weekends. Sometimes he used Matthew to make his victims feel comfortable. He showed them his son's toys in his truck. He brought them to his house. He showed them the boy's room. The women thought he was harmless. Then he choked them to death. He hid the bodies in the woods. Many times he went back and visited the dead bodies.

The number of killings skyrocketed. Police were confused. Soon authorities set up the Green River Task Force. This was a group of 50 or more detectives and helpers. They worked full time to find the Green River Killer. They went on TV. They asked people to call if they knew anything. Police got thousands of tips. The Green River Task Force followed up on each one. They combed every crime scene. They gathered every bit of evidence they could find.

Gary Ridgway's name kept coming up. Members of the task force interviewed him several times over the years. They could never pin anything on him.

Caught!

Police used *DNA* testing on the evidence in 2001. It was the break the task force had been waiting for. Scientists analyzed body fluid found on four girls killed 20 years earlier. It was Ridgway's. The police had him cold. The DNA and other evidence proved him guilty.

Police arrested Gary Ridgway on November 30, 2001. They picked him up while he was at work.

Gary Ridgway entered a *plea bargain* on November 5, 2003. He made a deal with the court. He admitted to the killings so that he would not be executed. He pleaded guilty to murdering 48 women. The court sentenced him to life in prison with no hope for parole. He told police where he had buried the bodies. That way the victims' families could move on.

Gary Ridgway is locked up at Washington State Penitentiary in Walla Walla, Washington.

GLOSSARY

appeal—a request for a new hearing

capital crime—a crime that can result in the death penalty

cremation—reducing a dead body to ashes by burning

death warrant—a paper that orders that an execution be carried out

decompose—to rot and fall apart

devastated—stunned, destroyed, overwhelmed

diamorphine—a legal type of heroin

DNA—deoxyribonucleic acid, the building blocks of life

domineering—bossy and mean

execute—to lawfully put someone to death for his or her crimes

exhume—to dig up a buried body in order to examine it

extradite—to take a person to another state to be tried for a crime committed there

GLOSSARY

fantasize—to imagine something happening

forgery—a fake document or signature

homophobic—fearful of, or hateful to, gay people

illegitimate—born to parents who are not married

indecent exposure—the crime of showing private parts to someone in public

infamous—having a very bad reputation

inmate—a prisoner in a jail or prison

lethal injection—a method of carrying out the death penalty with shots of poisonous drugs

meticulous—precise, fussy, thorough

plea bargain—an agreement where the accused pleads guilty to a lesser charge to avoid going to trial for a more serious charge

probate—laws having to do with the wills of people who have died

prosecutorial immunity—freedom from punishment, given in exchange for helping police prove a crime partner's guilt

suburban—located in the towns outside a big city

INDEX

INDEX